This **BLOOMSBURY** Activity Book belongs to:

_____

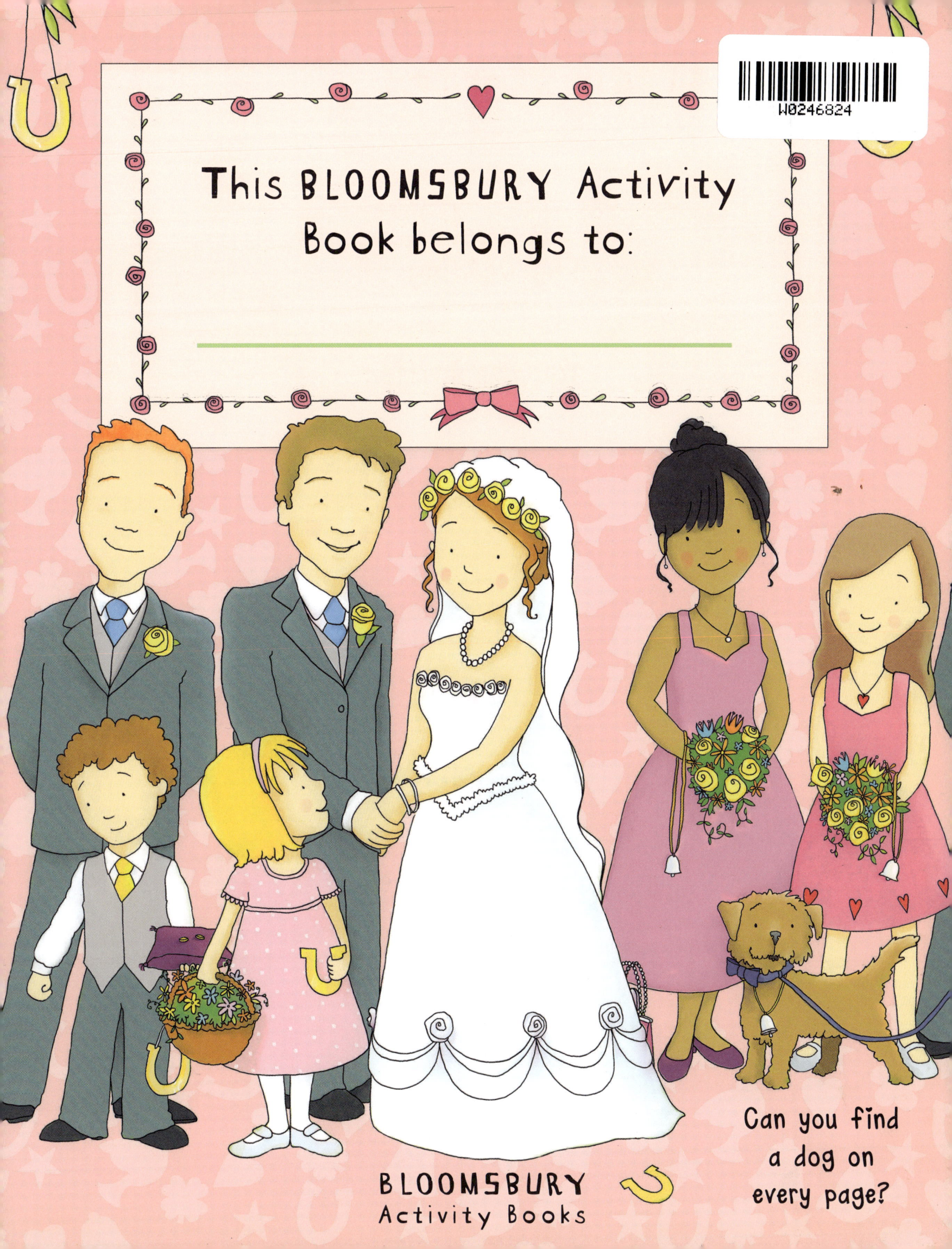

BLOOMSBURY
Activity Books

Can you find
a dog on
every page?

How it all started

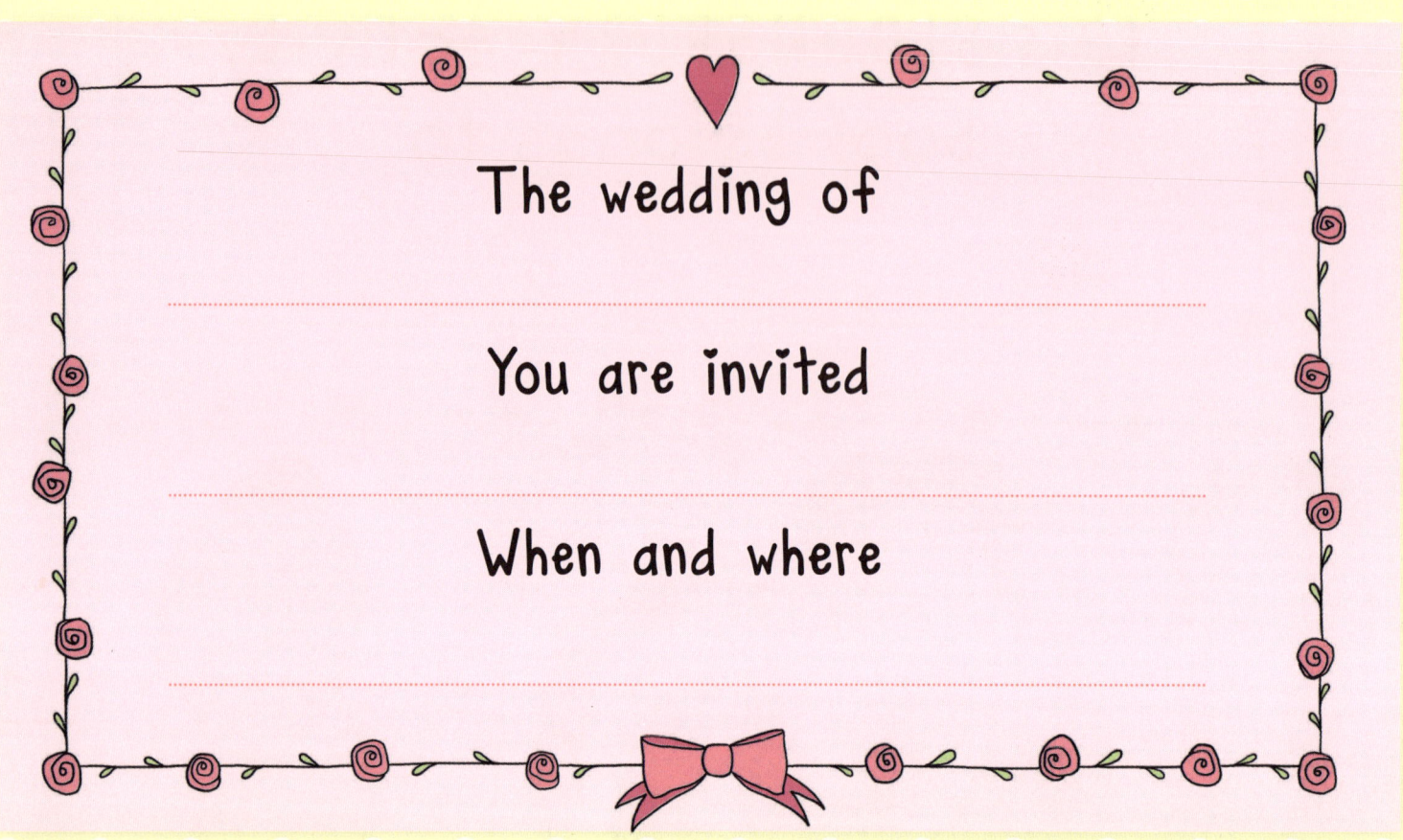

The wedding of

You are invited

When and where

The wedding of

You are invited

When and where

nvitations. Add sticker hearts, bows, bells, and flowers.
you are a princess. Who would you invite?

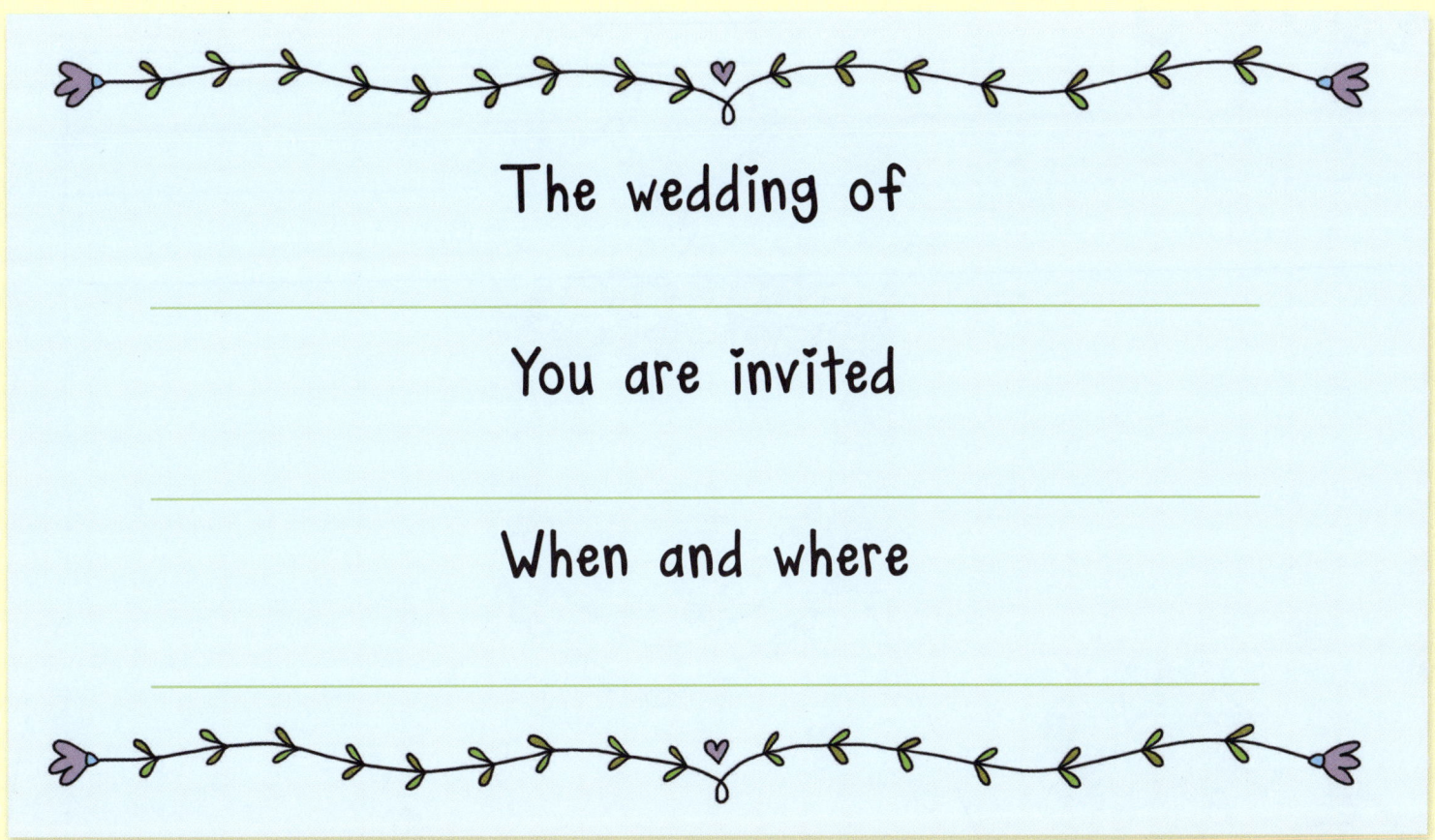

The wedding of

You are invited

When and where

The wedding of

You are invited

When and where

The beautiful wedding dress

Colour in this page.

Design your own dress. Add stickers to decorate the page.

Wedding day makeover

Draw a beautiful hairstyle on the bride with a glittering tiara and veil.

Give her some make-up and add some jewellery.

Draw a beautiful hairstyle on the bridesmaid with a headband made of flowers.

Give her some make-up and add some jewellery.

7

Who wears what?

Follow the ribbon paths to see who is wearing what.

9

The big day

Can you see 5 red hearts, 4 golden horseshoes, 3 silve

bells, 2 blue ties, and a pink bag in this picture?

11

What a pretty pair!

Match each flower girl to her page boy. The clues are in the colours and patterns, and what they are holding.

Flower power

Colour in the flowers so that the

natch the ones in the bouquets.

15

I can draw the bride and groom

16

Pages 2-3

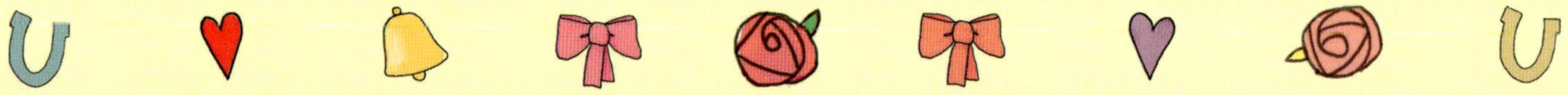

Pages 4-5

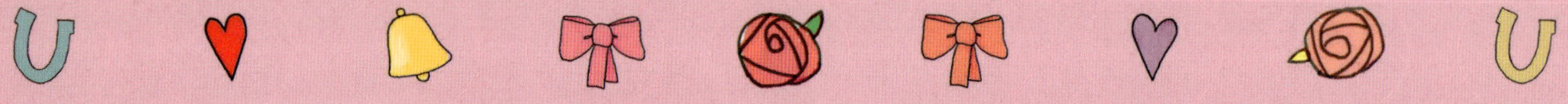

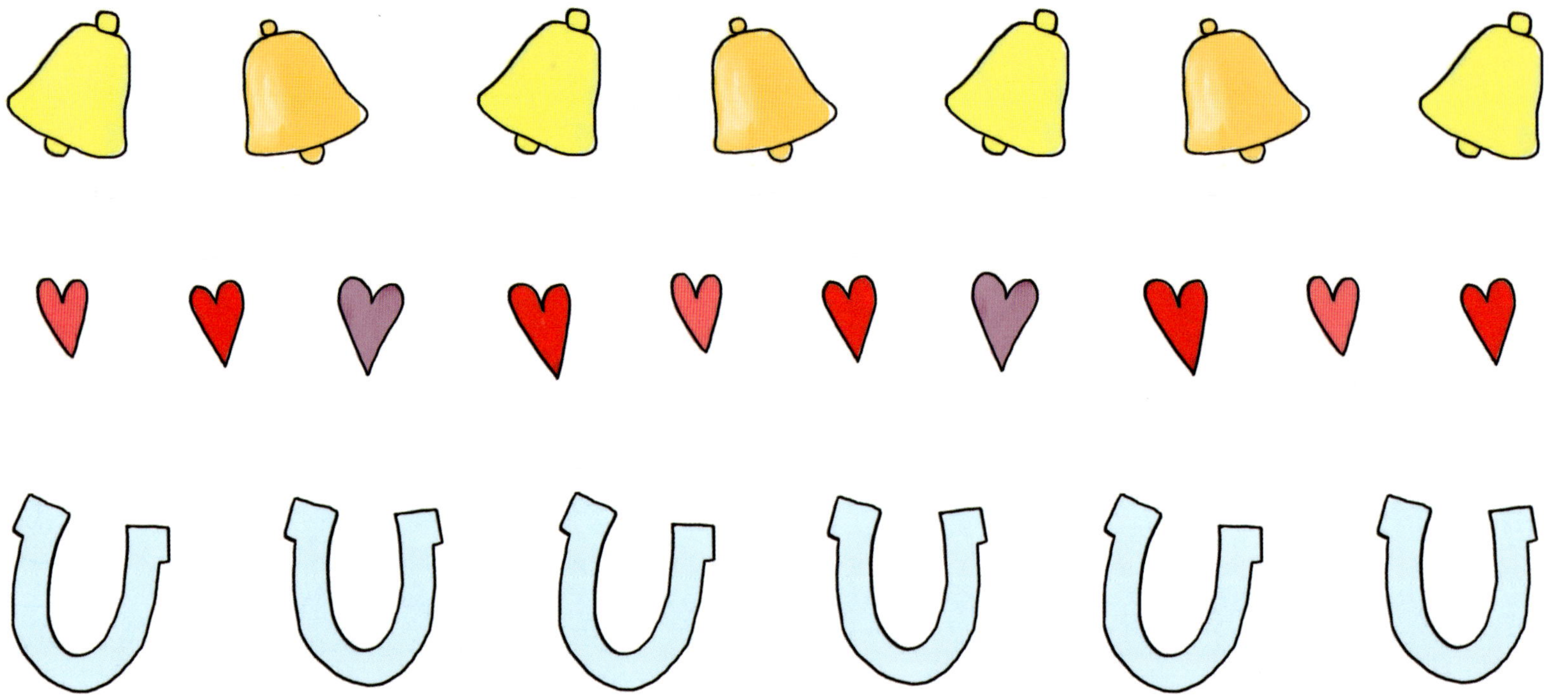

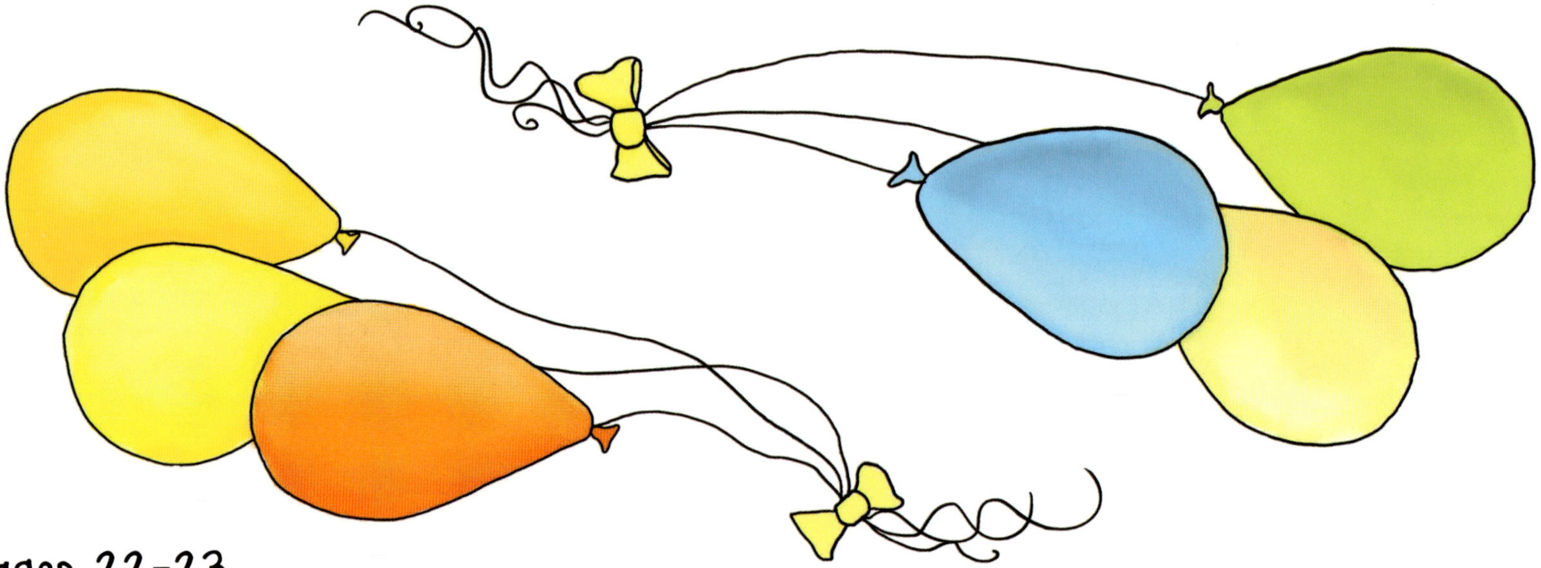

Pages 22-23

Page 29

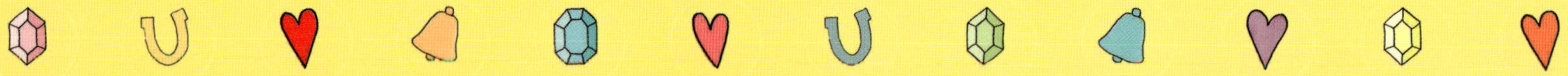

Using the grid as a guide, copy and colour
the bride and groom picture.

Spot the odd one out

Which is the odd-one-out in each group?

Paper rain

Colour in the confetti.

In the party tent

22

Decorate the tablecloth with stickers and add balloon stickers to the tent.

The wonderful feast

Find and colour all the folded napkins like this one.

Find the other
ice-creams like
this one and
colour them in.

25

Pretty patterns

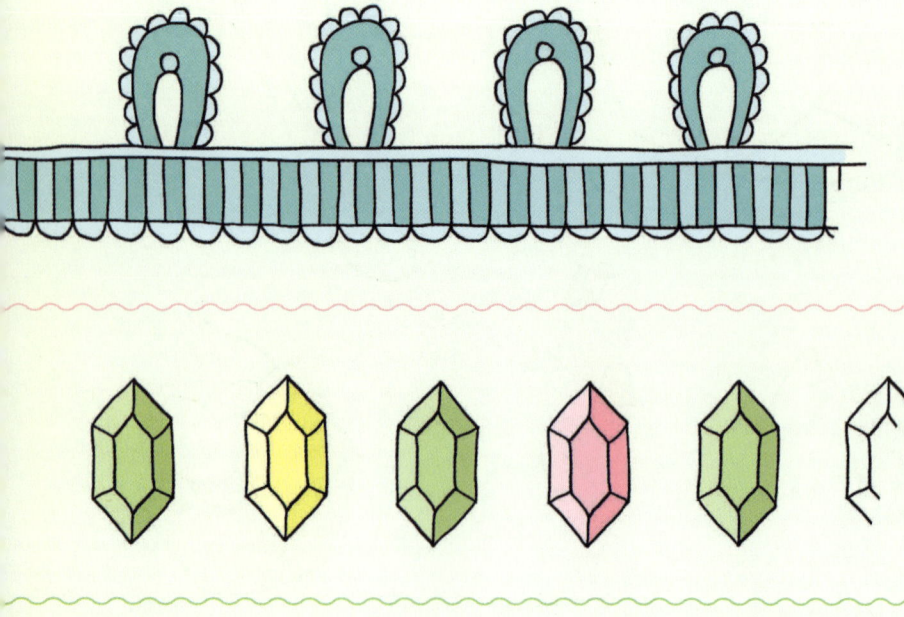

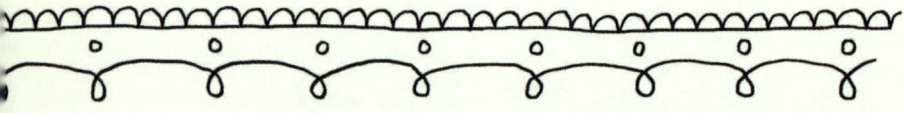

 26

Doodle, draw, and colour lace pattern

 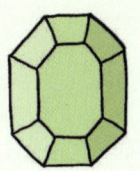

nd jewels across the pages.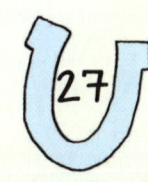

Time to cut the cake

Colour in the cake to match the card.

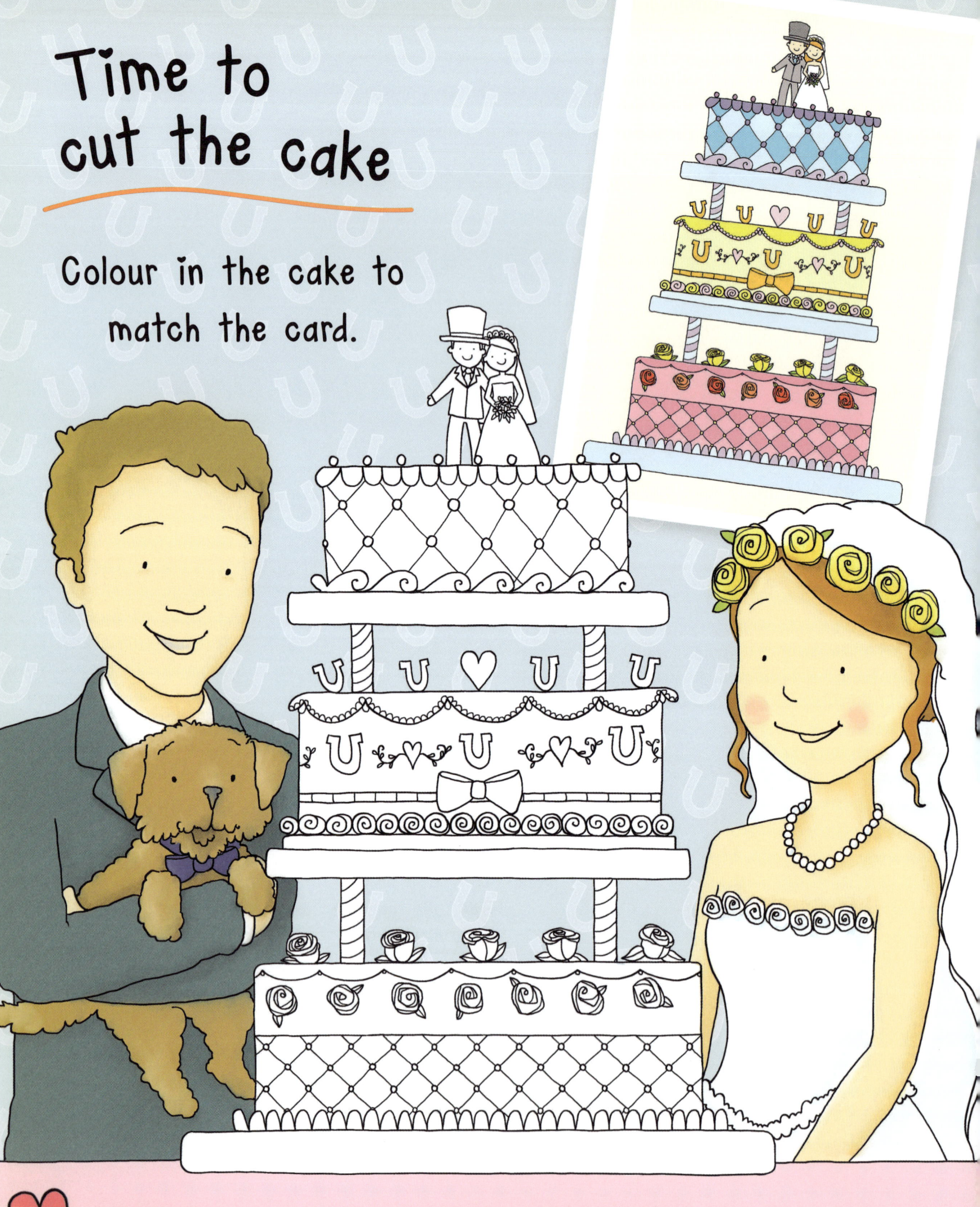

Use stickers to finish decorating
the wedding cupcakes.

29

Picture memories to keep

Draw pictures or add photographs of you at a wedding to the frames.

The end of the day

What are the page boy and
the flower girl dreaming about?